TOUGH SHIFT

Seriously Good Change

KEVIN W. MCCARTHY

AUTHOR *of* THE ON-PURPOSE PERSON

Published by Tremendous Leadership
PO Box 267 • Boiling Springs, PA 17007
(800) 233 - 2665 • *www.TremendousLeadership.com*

Tremendous Leadership's titles may be bulk purchased for business or promotional use or for special sales. Please contact Tremendous Leadership for more information.

ISBN-13 978-1-949033-64-9

Designed and Made in the United States of America

TOUGH SHIFT™

Contents

FYI

Get Your Free Downloads Now

These printable PDFs will enhance your TOUGH SHIFT learning experience.

1. TOUGH SHIFT Workbook (Use for Questions 1–7)
2. The On-Purpose Poster (Use for Questions 3–6)
3. The Discovery Guide (Use for Question 4)
4. Values List (Use for Question 6)
5. Preview of first four chapters of *The On-Purpose Person*

Download all for free at *TOUGHSHIFTtools.com* or scan the QR code:

Find Your 2-Word Purpose

(Use for Question 4)

ONPURPOSE.*me* is both the website address and the name of an online tool for finding your purpose in life. Included is a follow-up inspiring, instructional email series. Go to ONPURPOSE.*me* or scan the QR Code:

Contact Information

To inquire about TOUGH SHIFT programs and products, please visit *TOUGHSHIFT.com*

Hail to the mighty en-dash
Punctuating life in a flash
Flanked by year of birth-death
Representing first to last breath
"Punctuating Life"
Kevin W. McCarthy, 1954 –

TOUGH SHIFT: *Birth – Death*

The moment of your birth, you simultaneously took your first breath and experienced your first TOUGH SHIFT. Being expelled from the comfy womb into the cold air of a new world left you kicking and crying.

Charles, our son, distinguished his C-section birth with a yellow stream shooting an astounding four feet into the air! A quick-handed Dr. Morales, our high-risk pregnancy obstetrician, held a paste-covered, red-faced, crying Charles by his naked bottom in one hand and the back of his head in the other. With a deft, sweeping pivot, he aimed this fountain of youth toward an unoccupied corner of the operating room. The good-humored doctor turned to me and announced, "It's a boy. And it works!"

A TOUGH SHIFT Event is a particularly difficult life transition. If you aren't directly facing one of these disruptive events right now, then you most likely have friends, family, and colleagues who are. And that affects you.

Gold Nuggets

Scott Alexander's TOUGH SHIFT arrived as a cancer diagnosis. For 17 years, Scott's medical support company and my business, On-Purpose Partners, shared a lobby in a small, single-story office building. For four of those years, Scott and I were members of a small men's group that gathered in the building owner's conference room to discuss books about finances, life, business, family, and faith. Scott was an affable man with a keen mind, a kind spirit, and a strong belief in God.

I invited my then 84-year-old dad to a father-son outing. Late into Scott's battle with cancer, he spoke at an event on the "Gold Nuggets of Suffering." There, Scott shared about his six-year ordeal, including over 600 doctor appointments with more than 100 radiation treatments for more than 200 tumors. He endured a catalog of therapies and drugs in the faint hope of extending the length and quality of his life.

Rare are the times when we hear, let

alone walk beside, a dying man sharing lessons learned through pain and suffering. Instead of cursing as many would have done, Scott counted the blessings from his cancer. He said he experienced God's unconditional love, and, in turn, he gave greater love to others. Scott was terminal, but he chose to see the eternal.

Afterward, Dad said to me, "I have to shake Scott's hand." Upon introducing them, Dad said, "Scott, you're my hero!"

Five years later, Scott's "Gold Nuggets" prepared my father and comforted him through his dying process. Scott had shown us the power we have to choose to enter a hero's story, even in facing death.

Many see death as the enemy of life, but some, like Scott and Dad, embrace it as a necessary process to produce seeds of hope and inspiration. Death can be seen as the cold end or as the ultimate healing. Every TOUGH SHIFT you encounter throughout your life will involve making decisions. You choose.

Get Ready to Choose

You survived your first TOUGH SHIFT and have yet to face your final one. But what about the "mighty en-dash" that lies between birth and death? Having set the bookends for earthly living, let's concentrate on the remaining TOUGH SHIFTS that punctuate life.

Like ocean waves hitting a sandy beach, TOUGH SHIFTS overlap throughout our lives. Sometimes the "sea" is calm. Other times storm clouds gather, the water becomes choppy, and you can see a storm brewing in the distance with hurricane-force winds. You'll notice the warning signs—the growing push and pull of the tide, the churn of change. When this happens, you'll know you're in for a TOUGH SHIFT Event.

It isn't how a TOUGH SHIFT finds us; it's how we deal with it that counts. ☺

Adversity introduces a man to himself.

Albert Einstein, 1879 – 1955

What Is a TOUGH SHIFT Event?

A TOUGH SHIFT Event is the catalyst for a life transition. Like seasons in a year, they're inescapable yet essential to growth. The winds of change constantly swirl about us. Some can take years to develop. Others happen in an instant.

Positive or Negative

A *positive* TOUGH SHIFT Event is a cause for celebration. A desired change is often the culmination of active planning and pursuit, such as a goal met or a milestone achieved. Examples of a positive TOUGH SHIFT Event might be a graduation, job promotion, wedding, the start of a business, birth of a child, or retirement. We welcome these transitions into the rhythms and routines of our lives.

A *negative* TOUGH SHIFT Event, on the other hand, might include a divorce, firing, bankruptcy, illness, or death. These unexpected and unwanted situations often knock us to our knees or plunge us into chaos and confusion.

In addition, TOUGH SHIFT Events don't just happen in our personal lives; they happen in organizations, too, with changes such as new leadership, mergers, and competition. Team examples could include equipment failures, schedule changes, and budget cuts. Even at a governmental level, we can face TOUGH SHIFTS through elections, economic events, natural disasters, riots, war, and more.

Whew! Is it any wonder why life is overwhelming?

Fortunately, you're far more accustomed to and capable of accommodating a TOUGH SHIFT Event than you likely realize. Like breathing, it's easy to take this ability for granted. Then one TOUGH SHIFT Event, or a series of them, comes along and leaves you breathless, gasping for air and seeking relief.

Did you know that your point of view is the single greatest determinant for the outcome of a TOUGH SHIFT Event? Two people can contend with the same crises. Yet, their perspectives are what define their respective experiences as tough or not.

While identifying a TOUGH SHIFT Event, in and of itself, won't alter situations or your initial reactions to them, it does offer you a choice. Once you name it, you can either blame it, or you can tame it!

Blame It

As creatures of habit, we often resist change. Reaching for convenient weapons such as denial and blame, we fight with false security, only to end up mired in an ever-deepening pile of "shift," pointing our fingers at everyone but ourselves.

"Tough shit," the popular alternative phrase to TOUGH SHIFT, is a fatalistic vulgarity. It's a cruel curse and a terminal proclamation that nothing good can emerge from current circumstances. It halts hope and professes that life sucks. Such resignation amounts to a surrender of mind, body, spirit, or a combination thereof. Welcome to self-appointed victim status.

However, you have the choice of being a victor rather than a victim of your circumstances. Ultimately, you are your greatest advantage or disadvantage in life. It's your thoughts, feelings, beliefs, and attitudes that conspire for or against you. Be your own advantage!

As Einstein's quote above conveys, TOUGH SHIFT Events reveal your character to the world and, more importantly, to you. If you like what you see, build on it. If you don't like what emerges, you don't have to remain stuck in the swamp of negativity and despair.

Tame It

"TOUGH SHIFT" is not just a clever play on words for the title of this book. It's a descriptive turn of phrase to leverage to your advantage. The process presented in this book converts the vulgar "Tough Shit" into the virtue of a TOUGH SHIFT Mindset.

When the storms of TOUGH SHIFT Events turn your world upside down, the urgent can overwhelm the important. Doubt and despair may swirl like eddies seeking to sink a ship. The TOUGH SHIFT Process provides an anchor to what's truly important, building your resistance to recalibrate, restore, and revitalize.

Once you can say, "Oh, it's just a TOUGH SHIFT," your transformation has begun! ☺

To be able to ask a question clearly is two-thirds of the way to getting it answered.
John Ruskin, 1819 – 1900

What Is the TOUGH SHIFT Process?

The TOUGH SHIFT Process prepares and equips you to sort through the chaos of TOUGH SHIFT Events to get to a place of clarity. Rather than allowing you to sink into an emotional abyss, the TOUGH SHIFT Process provides you opportunities for phoenix-like renewal. It calls you to explore questions and discover answers about your worldview, identity, purpose, vision, missions, values, and contributions.

7 TOUGH SHIFT Questions

1. Is life meaningful?
2. Who am I?
3. Why do I exist?
4. Where am I going?
5. What "should" I do?
6. What's important?
7. How can I make a difference?

A mere three to six words long, each of these questions stands on its own. They're collectively synergistic. The rest of the book expands upon the 7 TOUGH SHIFT Questions. Addressing them in numerical order peels back layers of thought. The weight of each question ensures that the entirety of your efforts will be greater than the sum of the parts.

The centering effects of your answers ground your mind, quiet nagging thoughts, and set a new standard for your well-being. Choices anchored in thoughtfulness and discernment, instead of hunches or impulse, allow you to move forward with the necessary confidence, humor, and determination to transcend your present trial. The TOUGH SHIFT Process empowers you to chisel resilience into the masterpiece of your character.

Gaining Your Advantage

During your first time working through the 7 TOUGH SHIFT Questions, answer instinctively. An uncertain answer is better than an unanswered question because you gain an advantage over your old self with each stroke of your pen or keyboard. Regard this first set of answers as version 1.0.

As you encounter future TOUGH SHIFT Events, you will want to revisit the

TOUGH SHIFT Questions to revise your answers. With each easily repeatable cycle through the TOUGH SHIFT Process, you'll improve at separating who you are from what is happening to you.

Distancing gives you a healthier perspective to make sense of the circumstances and world around you. Versions 2.0, 3.0, and so forth will come more efficiently and effectively. Much like your computer or a smartphone operating system (OS), the TOUGH SHIFT Process codifies and documents your OS. Each new "release" offers a smarter, more experienced, more refined, and more capable you. Updates to fix bugs and add features and functionality provide ongoing improvements and causes for celebration instead of condemnation.

While it is true that errors in judgment hold consequences, they are often rich in redemptive capacity to resurrect a flourishing and fulfilled new life. Instead of insisting on a clean install, revisit each TOUGH SHIFT Question to analyze, deconstruct, and reconstruct your OS program. With time, your TOUGH SHIFT OS will become your trusted, on-call navigator that ignites your innermost strengths and guides you through stormy times.

In a cave of confusion, people can either stumble over rocks in the darkness or learn to mine jewels of greatness, like Scott Alexander's "Gold Nuggets of Suffering." Diamonds form with heat and pressure far below the earth's surface. So, too, character is forged in the crucible of this interior work. The TOUGH SHIFT Process provides a treasure map to the acres of diamonds within you.

At first, some of the TOUGH SHIFT Questions may seem impossible to answer. However, your answers will produce a sort of spiritual sonar to the depth of your soul. Will you find a foreboding passage hiding long-buried hurt and pain? Yes. Will you find the way to renewed life? Yes. Like any great adventure, there is risk and reward. Fear not! While you can certainly anticipate challenges on this journey, you control just how deep and far you'll take it.

What's at stake? Every decision in your life is influenced in whole or in part by some combination of your answers to these questions. The return on investment of your time, thought, and energy from answering these foundational 7 TOUGH SHIFT Questions is priceless. While it carries zero assurance of a perfect life, the TOUGH SHIFT Process offers the reality of personal growth.

Your answers are within you. Enter the TOUGH SHIFT Process expecting the true you to emerge.

Ready, Set, Go! 😉

I shall be telling this with a sigh
Somewhere ages and ages hence:
Two roads diverged in a wood, and I—
I took the one less traveled by,
And that has made all the difference.
"The Road Not Taken" (last stanza)
Robert Frost, 1874 – 1963

Question 1: Is Life Meaningful?

Apart from lying on the ground on summer evenings and gazing into the stars wondering about the meaning of life, Question 1 might seem like a luxury in your busy life. Sensing there's no way to know the answer, your mind may be drawn to more concrete and immediate questions like, *What's for dinner?*

Is life meaningful? As deeply philosophical as the question is, there are only two choices. What's your gut response? Mouth the words: Yes or No?

Regardless of your choice, no one can prove you right or wrong. Certainly, many will advocate their positions with resources and references, but, ultimately, no one has indisputable evidence to solve this age-old mystery.

What's left? Opinions. Perhaps even strongly held ones. But actual proof? Not possible. On this plane in the space-time continuum, some mysteries of life remain unsolved.

Either way you choose, it's an act of faith—confidence in the unknown. What is known is that your opinion forms your worldview, and your worldview dramatically shapes your life experiences.

With an appreciative nod to Robert Frost, which "road" will you take? Remember that your instinctive answer to Question 1 is your first, but not necessarily your final, opinion.

For decades I've asked people this question. About one-fifth of the respondents feel confident in their answers. The remaining 80% fall into the mushy middle ground. Let's unwrap the two possible answers so you can more accurately decide where you stand on this question.

Yes.

Many "Life is Meaningful" ideologies use terms like Higher Power, Supreme Being, The Universe, Intelligent Design, or the names of specific deities to acknowledge the existence of something or someone larger or more powerful than people. For simplicity and inclusion, let's call this unknown presence "God."

In surveys about Question 1, respondents chose the following words to characterize their "Life is Meaningful" beliefs:

Nouns: *design, creator, rules, purpose, order, hope, beauty, heaven, spirit, afterlife, service, generosity, reason, faith, ethics, mystery, structure, pattern*

Adjectives: *predictable, structured, boring, energizing, exhausting, restless, confusing, sacred, spiritual*

Concepts: *personal responsibility, accountability, cause and effect, good and evil*

No.

Numerous groups hold that "Life is Meaningless." For example, Existentialists might sum up their philosophy with, "Life is meaningless, but do good anyway." Famous philosophers such as Kierkegaard, Dostoevsky, Sartre, Camus, and Nietzsche advocate that the search for meaning in a meaningless universe is a fool's errand and that only the individual can assign meaning. In other words, forget the pursuit of purpose and get on with living. In fact, "Existence precedes essence" is about as close to doctrine as one finds within this line of thinking. Other mottoes could be "Live in the moment," "Seize the day," or "Nothing matters."

In surveys about Question 1, respondents characterized the "Life is Meaningless" mentality with the following descriptors:

Nouns: *pessimism, despair, chaos, beauty, freedom*

Adjectives: *random, scary, spontaneous, free-flowing, unpredictable, confusing, energizing, exhausting, restless, incredible, absurd, amoral, unfair, uncaring*

Concepts: *no personal responsibility, no accountability, no cause and effect, no control, no purpose, no rules, no religion, no creator, no hope, no meaning, no afterlife*

You can see that both sets of respondents agree that life is beautiful and energizing but also restless, exhausting, and confusing. However, the "Life is Meaningful" respondents and the "Life is Meaningless" respondents could not have more differing perspectives on concepts like personal responsibility, accountability, cause and effect, hope, creation, and an afterlife.

Having written *The On-Purpose Person: Making Your Life Make Sense*, I'll disclose that I stand on the side of meaning. Why? While a TOUGH SHIFT Event can temporarily make life appear meaningless, meaning always emerges in time. It brings with it the potential to grow character, improve well-being, and increase leadership abilities. Only meaningfulness allows for this possibility of hope as opposed to absolute hopelessness.

Your Final Answer?

Go back and review each word list above. Which set of descriptors best aligns with your beliefs? Is your answer now the same as your gut response from earlier? At least for the benefit of this exercise and the next six questions, pick an answer and record it in your downloaded *TOUGH SHIFT Workbook*. (If you haven't yet downloaded your free copy of the workbook, this is a good time to do that. See the FYI at the beginning of the book for details.)

Still unsure in your response? In this instance, a waffling answer doesn't serve your best interest. Indulge me and give the "Life is Meaningful" way a chance for TOUGH SHIFT Questions 2–7. Think about it, if everything is meaningless, then this book and its questions are meaningless. Why waste your time in a meaningless pursuit? As you work through the remaining questions, it is my earnest desire that you feel you have used your time wisely.

Your worldview makes a world of difference. ☺

Once a profound truth has been seen, it cannot be "unseen."
There's no "going back" to the person you were.
Even if such a possibility did exist … why would you want to?
Dave Sim, 1956 –

Question 2: Who Am I?

TOUGH SHIFTS can easily pierce many a protective façade to expose the good, bad, and ugly of who we are on the inside. Quickly, we discover if our inner lives are shallow or deep.

Each TOUGH SHIFT Event we experience adds missing pieces to the jigsaw puzzle of identity. In youth, we work to put the edges in place. Then, with the frame formed, we add internal "pieces" to understand the bigger picture.

Helen, a friend, volunteers at a hospice facility. I asked, "Isn't being with terminally ill patients depressing?"

Helen smiled, "Hardly. Comfort care is my calling. I have two types of patients: those with and those without pretense. Those who drop their pretenses are real and experience a full range of emotions. Conversations are remarkably raw and penetrating. I have the privilege to meet the true person. Why do so many of us wait to live until we're dying?"

Do You Identify?

The greatest obstacle to knowing oneself is confusing identifiers with identity.

Imagine that you enter a party. Your host greets you and asks you to write your name on one of those "Hello, I am...." name tags. You jot down your name and apply the sticker to your shirt.

Now people know you. Really? Your name is an identifier, but it's not your identity. What's the difference?

Identifiers are descriptions conveying affinity. For example, people tout, "I'm Italian" or "southern" or "from the Bronx" as if that explains who they are. Wearing a team jersey declares allegiance. Designer labels send status signals. Ford or Chevy? The list goes on—mostly in good fun!

Some see identity as mystical. Words such as psyche, spark, essence, spirit, and soul can be considered close proxies. Your identity, however, consists of your unique, intangible presence "found" in knowing your purpose, character, personality, gifts, attitudes, preferences, experiences, and more.

TOUGH SHIFT Events both expose and forge identity. Maturity is the process of coming to know, like, and trust yourself so you're "comfortable in your own skin." In contrast, a person described as a poser, fake, phony, or lost soul may not really "know who they are." The question becomes, "How do you consistently and authentically be your best self?"

Mistaken Identity

People often spend their lives in misguided forages for identity and inadvertently reinforce the "Life is Meaningless" worldview. Faulty sourcing for your identity produces faulty results. Three commonly misplaced sources of identity include people, things, and activities. Each is a perilous and pointless origin of identity.

Identity found in another person eventually forms bitter codependency. For example, if my identity comes from my spouse, I risk being controlling or being controlled. Love, honor, and respect, but don't idolize.

Identity tethered to perishable items

such as cars, money, and clothing leads to a shallow and insecure existence. A frail need to "be somebody" through possessions breeds ethical compromises. It's OK to want things, except as the basis of your existence.

Identity anchored in activity yields defensive arrogance. The classic example of confusing who we are with what we do produces an emotional roller coaster ride that disembarks in isolation and ruin. The unchallengeable know-it-all may be "right" while still getting it all wrong and winding up alone. Reject this pretension or it will consume you.

I Am . . .

God, our inclusive term, is the only healthy origin for identity and existence. Until you know who God is, you can't know who you are meant to be. Even then, sourcing your identity in God is a challenge of trust requiring an act of faith.

You've learned from Question 1 that life is meaningful and from Question 2 where to source your answer; but you still don't have an answer to Question 2. Wait—help is on the way. Question 3 will point you in the right direction.

When the "true you" surfaces, you'll know it. 😉

Things can be really empty in this world, and I don't just mean the music world. It can become a very meaningless place if you don't really understand: "Who am I? Why am I here? What am I doing?" To feel fulfillment and have a deeper level of understanding, personally, that is the most important thing.

Alicia Keys, 1981 –

Question 3: Why Do I Exist?

Remaining largely unanswered through millennia, this question points to finding one's purpose.

In his book *Man's Search for Meaning*, Dr. Viktor Frankl recounts his captivity in a Nazi concentration camp. This experience produced his life's work called *Logotherapy*, a psychological approach based on three key tenets:

1. Life has meaning even in the worst of conditions and circumstances.

2. The search for the meaning of life is the primary motivator in people.

3. Each person possesses the freedom to find meaning in their experiences even in the face of radical hardship.

Dr. Frankl provides insights into what is meaningful, but not a specific answer to the question at hand. He does, however, narrow the search radius for finding identity and purpose.

Answering this TOUGH SHIFT Question can be risky business because it's a call to be counter-cultural. Cultural norms are typically built, reinforced, and rewarded by purposeless drifters in the majority thrashing in their seas of meaninglessness. Their energetic fight and cries of foul play aim to pull others down into the drowning despair of mindless mediocrity. We must not let ourselves get swept away.

Submission is almost always easier than resistance. Paradoxically, sticking to the norm seems simple, even though it is less secure. Resistance, on the other hand, a perilous path. For people who have only known the life of a purpose-searcher and not a purpose-owner, the risk-reward gap often appears too wide and difficult to cross. Purpose seems an impractical indulgence when the bills are due. But discovering your purpose pushes you out of your comfort zone to resist the natural in favor of the supernatural.

"Who am I to live a supernatural life?" you ask. This inflection point potentially marks the start of a positive TOUGH SHIFT in your lifeline. Yet, arguably, this lifelong battle may be one of the most difficult of your life, a war for your soul between the mundane and the magnificent.

But don't worry; you're not alone. After all, "It's just a TOUGH SHIFT."

Purpose Unlocked

When speaking to groups, Corrie ten Boom, another Holocaust survivor and author of *The Hiding Place*, often worked needlepoint. As she spoke, her audience could only see the knotted, stringy side of the stitching. Near the end, she would flip over her blue fabric to reveal a gold crown. Similarly, your purpose flips the script of your life. Instead of just seeing the messy, your awakened eyes see the masterpiece.

Remember that whenever you embrace a TOUGH SHIFT, transformation is on the horizon. The positive TOUGH SHIFT of discovering your purpose offers you a key. Will you unlock the door, open it, and step across the threshold into an abundance of possibilities, purpose, and promise?

The pivotal scene in Disney's movie *The Lion King* finds Simba, the protagonist, wallowing in self-pity. Mistakenly believing that he is to blame for his father's death, Simba had detached himself from responsibility and, like the prodigal son of the Bible, had high-tailed it to frolic with friends. After listening to Simba's grumbling for long enough, Rafiki the priestly baboon swiftly smacks Simba on the head with his rod. A miffed Simba asks, "What was that for?"

"It doesn't matter. It is in the past," Rafiki retorts.

Rubbing his skull, Simba replies, "Yeah, but it still hurts."

"Ah, yes, the past can hurt," explains the wise primate. "But the way I see it, you can either run from it … or learn from it." He takes another swing at Simba who deftly dodges the stick. Lesson learned.

Purpose Lost?

"If my purpose is who I am, and I am just now figuring out my purpose, then I've wasted my life up to now." Avoid such conclusions that are fraught with regret.

Take heart! Purpose redeems your past. All the lessons and experiences that have shaped you into the imperfect person you are today are instructive for rehabilitating your future.

If necessary to move forward, forgive yourself for not knowing what you didn't know before you knew your purpose. While you're at it, forgive others of their wrongdoings, too. We're all on a learning curve toward maturity and decency. Be tenderhearted and thick-skinned instead of thin-skinned and hard-hearted.

Purpose Found

Your past has passed. Your present and future are in play.

With the ONPURPOSE.*me* online tool listed on the FYI page at the front of this book, you can discover your 2-word purpose within minutes. Take the time to do this, then ask yourself again, "Why do I exist?" Your response will now begin with, "I exist to serve by...." It will end with two words—your purpose.

While your 2-word purpose offers you the upper hand, it only partially equips you to step boldly toward victory. Answering TOUGH SHIFT Questions 4–7 will prepare you to better appreciate your past and welcome your future with courage and conviction.

The gift of purpose is yours to unwrap and present to the world! 😉

Whatever the mind can conceive and believe, it can achieve.
Napoleon Hill, 1883 – 1970

Question 4: Where Am I Going?

This question is answered in your mind's eye. If you can't visualize where you're going, you're unlikely to get there in real life. Dreams, wants, wishes, ideals, and hopes are all words that might pop into your head here. But because the answer to this question is actionable and obtainable, vision is the most accurate term. Conceived in your spirit, but born, raised, and realized in your mind, vision tells you where you're going.

A TOUGH SHIFT Event and lack of vision are all too common companions. For high achievers, obtaining "the goal," such as winning an award, reaching the summit, or becoming a multimillionaire, often creates a vision void. "Now what?" Untethered to a specific plan, previously well-ordered lives can devolve into chaos.

At the other extreme, we find those cursed with the "loser" label. This misbranding haunts their thoughts with their fallback "vision" being one of a failure.

In either situation, lack of vision breeds discontentment.

As the Cheshire cat tells Alice in Lewis Carroll's book *Alice in Wonderland*, "If you don't know where you are going, any road will get you there."

The antidote to such meaningless meandering is to envision yourself as an "on-purpose person in creation." An "on-purpose person" is called to a purpose as opposed to driven by it, and to be "in creation" is to choose to be a lifelong learner and leader who willingly takes chances to experience life more fully. A clear vision provides positive direction; and a work-in-process mindset frees you to experiment your way to improvement and achievement.

Thomas Edison certainly embraced this attitude. When asked about his many attempts to create the light bulb, his classic reply was something like, "I haven't failed 1,000 times. I haven't failed once! I have succeeded in finding 1,000 ways that will not work. And when I've eliminated all the ways that don't work, I will find the way that does work."

Clarification

Vision can be thought of as a physical, mental, or spiritual waypoint. You will want to clarify a vision for each facet of your life: physical, vocational, financial, family, social, mental, spiritual, and perhaps educational. These sub-visions are called Life Accounts, and each contributes to a larger life vision.

Because most of us carry aspirations, "Where am I going?" tends to be the easiest to answer of all the TOUGH SHIFT Questions.

Use the questions below to prime the pump of your visioning process:

What character qualities do I aspire to be?

Who's my role model?

What does being healthy mean to me?

What's the best college for me to attend?

What's my dream job?

What does it look like to excel in my job, favorite sport, or hobby?

How much savings leaves me feeling financially independent?

Answering these questions can conjure favorable images. Writing down your answers or creating a vision board will further solidify where you are going.

What Do You Want?

A more comprehensive method for clarifying your vision is to use the Want List and Tournament techniques found in *The On-Purpose Person*. This is explained in *The Discovery Guide* at *TOUGHSHIFTtools.com* (as referenced on the FYI page at the beginning of the book.) For each Life Account, plan to invest 10 to 15 minutes for your vision, priorities, and values to surface. This purging and clarification of your wants will be well worth your time.

The Want List and Tournament technique comes in handy in a variety of interesting ways. When my children were under ten, we developed a Want List entitled, "What to do over the summer?" After coming up with 16 different ideas, we utilized the Tournament to settle on building a treehouse. We picked a backyard tree and researched tree house designs and building methods. Within a couple of weeks, they were loving their new play space.

A vision clarified is a vision cast. 😉

We must all suffer from one of two pains: the pain of discipline or the pain of regret. The difference is discipline weighs ounces while regret weighs tons.
Jim Rohn, 1930 – 2009

Question 5: What "Should" I Do?

Once a vision is cast, it can be planned. Once planned, it can be implemented. This leads us to Question 5. The answer to this question is your mission. Missions are what we do, not who we are. They fail or succeed, but the inherent worth of the person remains unaffected. Missions are intentional activities, each with a measurable start and finish, planned to express purpose while advancing a clear vision consistent within stated values.

Like Russian nesting dolls, missions contain plans, goals, projects, jobs, and tasks. A mission is an overall objective or assignment to be completed. Within the mission is a plan with specific goals marking progress. Plans include projects needed to complete different phases of the plan. Within a project are jobs for a person or team to deliver in accordance with standards such as due dates, quantity, quality, and cost. The innermost nesting doll represents an individual's task within a job.

TOUGH "Should"

This circles us back to the TOUGH SHIFT Question at hand: "What 'should' I do?" I am asked this question regularly in my consulting and advisory roles. I often reply, "Don't 'should' on yourself."

You probably noticed that "should" is in quotation marks. This highlights not only another play on words but also the error of its way. Whenever we use the word "should" in a question, we defer our agency to act to the person we are asking. "Should" essentially delegates our decision-making capability to another, asking them to own a mission that is not necessarily theirs.

"Shoulding" not only shifts responsibility to others, it shifts blame, as well, by implying someone "should" have known better. Anyone can criticize, tear down, or put down, but that's a self-deceiving blame game worth avoiding. In other words, don't "should" on yourself or on anyone else.

When working through a TOUGH SHIFT, embrace your authority to act. Take 100% responsibility to be engaged in creating a positive outcome. If you need to seek advice, ask, "What do you recommend?" Do your research, compare options, and do what's necessary to make informed decisions: right, wrong, or indifferent. If you don't, you'll likely pay a high price later.

In the 1980 movie *The Blues Brothers*, Jake and Elwood were "on a mission from God." So are you! Drop the "should" and ask "What will I do?"

The Second Moment

Purpose, vision, and mission are akin to the marksman's order of, "Ready, Aim, Fire." Mission is where the action is, but you can't skip over purpose and vision. They are prerequisite to the mission. When caught in the crosshairs of a TOUGH SHIFT, your impulse may be to act first. But know that, "Fire, Aim, Ready" is a reckless mistake.

Instead, devote a "second moment" to reflect on context and process. When you take time to sort the many possibilities, you will be more prepared to respond to any TOUGH SHIFT Event that comes your way.

Imagine a tennis player who must react to an opponent's serve. Training, experience, and fast reflexes ready the player to neutralize the serve.

Preparation for a TOUGH SHIFT is one of the secrets to skillfully navigating them. Periodically updating your 7 TOUGH SHIFT Answers offers a solid return on your time, energy, and resources. An added dividend is you're more likely to remain calm and composed in your next TOUGH SHIFT.

Having completed the Want List and Tournament for Question 4, search your forms for actionable items. Write these down in brainstorming. Connect the dots between purpose, vision, and mission so that they are aligned and on-purpose.

Own your mission. And, most importantly, "Don't 'should' on yourself!" 😉

The first principle of value that we need to rediscover is this: that all reality hinges on moral foundations. In other words, that this is a moral universe, and that there are moral laws of the universe just as abiding as the physical laws. ... But I'm not so sure if we know that there are, are moral laws, just as abiding as the physical law. I'm not so sure about that. I'm not so sure we really believe that there is a law of love in this universe, and that if you disobey it you'll suffer the consequences.

"Rediscovering Lost Values"

Sermon at Second Baptist Church, Detroit, Michigan, February 28, 1954

Martin Luther King, Jr., 1929 – 1968

Question 6: What's Important?

What's important is what you value. What you value is based on your values. If you don't know your values, you don't know what's important. Ill-defined values lead to being distractible, indecisive, compliant, and reckless. Yikes!

You already have values; everyone does. They are a set of principles or standards of behavior used consciously or unconsciously for making decisions. Like traffic lights, values signal green, yellow, or red.

Values can be moral and immoral. For example, "Family first" seems like a moral value. But, what if the family is the Mafia, and the Godfather thinks you're a snitch? An interpretation of that value might be, "You cross da family, you die!"

Purpose precedes values, as in Purpose, Vision, Mission, Values (**PVMV**). Purpose, by definition, is absolute good, whereas values are culturally subjective. A person who has a positive purpose, clear vision, and honorable mission, but lousy values will cause trouble. In the U.S. Armed Forces, such a violation of values often ends in a dishonorable discharge.

The Ethical Tiebreaker

Sometimes values may conflict. Therefore, purpose becomes your ethical tiebreaker. Absent a good purpose, values can be easily exploited or abused. Bad guys prey on the helpless by twisting good people's values. Conversely, clarity of PVMV hones shrewd discernment.

A man in an On-Purpose workshop once flagged me down to ask, "I'm down to two choices: buy a boat or put braces on my 12-year-old son. What should I do?"

Though my "should" meter beeped, I bit my tongue. "Tell me what you're thinking," I coached. For me it seemed like a no-brainer—invest in the kid's teeth.

"My son needs braces," he explained. "His teeth aren't that bad, but they could be a problem down the road."

"And the boat?" I probed.

"At 12 years old, we don't have many years left together to boat, fish, and just hang out. I want to create lifetime memories with him—and his friends."

Introducing the tiebreaker, I asked, "What's your 2-word purpose statement?"

"Imparting Wisdom." He smiled as he recognized, "Oh, it's the boat because it's relational."

The Time Management Deception

My book *FIT 4 Leading* is based on a survey of 852 small business owners who were asked, "What's your greatest obstacle to success?" The top response (32%) was "time management." To me, that's a smoke screen for saying, "I don't know what's important. Therefore, I do it all."

Allocating time, talent, and treasure without stated values diffuses focus and wastes resources while increasing stress. When your values are vague, your backbone is weak. Your compromised operating system becomes a magnet for negative TOUGH SHIFTS. You might think you're cursed, but you're simply adrift not knowing what truly matters.

Flip Wilson, twentieth-century comedian and host of the TV show bearing his name, coined the quip, "The devil made me do it." The absurdity of the humorous excuse to disassociate from one's bad choices made people laugh, but that doesn't mean you can blame others for your weak value woes. Blame never negates a wrong and typically makes matters worse.

According to Socrates, "The unexamined life is not worth living." If you're still mired in the malaise of mediocrity, examine your values for what's working and what isn't. Confer with a person you hold in high regard for their character to discuss and refine your PVMV.

Uncovering Your Values

The Want List and Tournament process is one of several ways to uncover your values. If you've already done this exercise, review each bracket to spot important patterns in your decisions. Make this your first set of values.

Alternatively, *TOUGHSHIFTtools.com* includes a list of personal values to speed forming your first list. Over time, refine your values. In days to come, you'll be thankful you stated your values today. ☺

A hero is someone who has given his or her life to something bigger than oneself.
Joseph Campbell, 1904 – 1987

Question 7: How Can I Make a Difference?

Your birth was a TOUGH SHIFT Event for you and for those who cared for you. Right from the womb you made a difference—and it continues. Never take this naked truth for granted.

"Making a Difference" could be the title song of the longings of our hearts for meaning. That desire to make a difference comes from noble character yearning to serve others. However, this soulful burning can be extinguished under layers of unprocessed TOUGH SHIFTS. Avoid raising the white flag of surrender and saying, "This is as good as life gets." Reject any such TOUGH SHIFT (without the "F") mentality.

Focus instead on this truth: "What you sow is what you reap." This principle is at work in your body, mind, and spirit to encourage contributing to the common good. Planting the TOUGH SHIFT Process in the fertile soil of your mind teaches you how to dig for hope and positive resolution in even the most adverse set of circumstances.

The Moment of Truth

In the classic 1946 movie *It's a Wonderful Life*, Jimmy Stewart plays the distraught George Bailey. When George's father unexpectedly dies of a stroke, George returns home to close the family business. TOUGH SHIFT. Intrigue ensures. TOUGH SHIFT Event after TOUGH SHIFT Event leads George to the rails of a bridge preparing to jump.

Fortunately, Clarence appears just in time. This apprentice angel shows George a dark and disturbing vision of what his hometown would be like if George had never lived. Realizing the difference his life is making, George's heart fills with gratitude as he heads back to his home, family, and responsibilities.

Fixing your attention on the difference you are NOT making causes distress. Counter this overshadowing by regularly practicing your TOUGH SHIFT Process.

Uniquely Called

Having settled that you are already making a difference, ask a more precise question: "How am I uniquely making a difference?"

In arithmetic, a difference is the remainder after subtraction. Pruning frees you to focus on and flourish in service to God, self, and others. What needs to go so you can get on with your unique calling? Instead of being a mile wide and an inch deep become the opposite: an inch wide and a mile deep. Depth of character earns respect.

Andrew Carnegie advised, "I tell you 'put all your eggs in one basket, and then watch that basket.' Look round you and take notice; men who do that do not often fail. It is easy to watch and carry the one basket. It is trying to carry too many baskets that breaks most eggs in this country. He who carries three baskets must put one on his head, which is apt to tumble and trip him up. One fault of the American businessman is lack of concentration."

"Kevin, we make money," the CEO of a multibillion-dollar company said to me once, "but what's our crusade?"

Borrowing that question, ask yourself, "What's my crusade?"

Crusades originate in purpose and gain form and function by activating vision, missions, and values. They're often revealed through a series of TOUGH SHIFTS patched together to form the quilt of a cause.

Sometimes, a TOUGH SHIFT can thrust a crusade upon us. The abduction and murder of 6-year-old Adam Walsh spurred his father to advocate for victims of violent crimes. John Walsh hosted the acclaimed TV show *America's Most Wanted* for 23 years, a calling that found him through tragedy.

Other times, relatable TOUGH SHIFTS bring people together for crusades. For example, Alcoholics Anonymous relies upon recovering alcoholics guiding other alcoholics. What heartbreaking TOUGH SHIFT so ignites your passion that you'll pay the price to make things right?

My personal crusade is eradicating meaninglessness. Decades of diverse life experiences, education, and entrepreneurship, plus client work, prepared me to declare war on this spiritual cancer.

Your 2-word purpose is a "vaccine" of pivotal importance. Instead of spending your life searching for meaning, you can productively invest it by giving expression to your purpose.

Crusades exist in three states with three distinct strategies:

1. **Unknown:** Do what is right and right in front of you.

2. **Emerging:** Discern to the core.
3. **Known:** Act boldly!

Finding yourself in state one or two? Review your TOUGH SHIFT Answers 1-6 to uncover your unique contribution.

Phillips Brooks, a nineteenth-century clergyman, wrote in *Purpose and Use of Comfort*, "Greatness after all, in spite of its name, appears to be not so much a certain size as a certain quality in human lives. It may be present in lives whose range is very small."

What's small? My friend Rosemary volunteered to work a month with Mother Teresa at a Missionaries of Charity home for the dying. Her first Calcutta encounter with the venerable nun wasn't in a posh office but at the bedside of a dying man Mother Teresa held. Any great movement relies upon the intimacy found in person-to-person relationships where the little deal becomes the big deal.

The book of Zechariah teaches, "Do not despise these small beginnings, for the LORD rejoices to see the work begin, to see the plumb line in Zerubbabel's hand." Your purpose is your plumb line. Use it.

Start small, think big, be a hero. 😉

Strength does not come from winning. Your struggles develop your strengths. When you go through hardships and decide not to surrender, that is strength.
Arnold Schwarzenegger, 1947 –

TOUGH SHIFT and Leadership

Anyone can destroy. Leaders create through positive TOUGH SHIFTS. Regardless of whether you start a business, paint a picture, write a book, exercise your body, or innumerable other examples of creating, you've decided to overcome the natural gravity of decay.

Leading is countercultural. Disengagement and apathy befriend the status quo and prevent progress. To the contrary, strong leaders muster the courage and capacity to overcome inertia and risk failure. The antidote to a devastating TOUGH SHIFT is a positive TOUGH SHIFT.

In 1937, Don Budge became the first winner of the tennis Grand Slam. He stated, "I lost lots of matches to learn how to win matches."

Similarly, legend Michael Jordan shares, "I've missed more than 9,000 shots in my career. I've lost almost 300 games. Twenty-six times, I've been trusted to take the game-winning shot and missed. I've failed over and over and over again in my life. And that is why I succeed."

Victory and loss, as with joy and sadness, must coexist for each to be appreciated.

"Nothing in life is to be feared, it is only to be understood." Let these words from Marie Curie inspire you, "Now is the time to understand more, so that we may fear less."

Answering the 7 TOUGH SHIFT Questions means you "understand more" so you will "fear less." Give fear no home in your heart!

Celebrate how far you've come in clarifying your worldview, discovering who you are, and understanding why you exist. You have stated your purpose, vision, mission, and values. Embrace being a difference maker in service to God, self, and others. At no one else's expense, you have gained an advantage to meaningfully engage in the world while continuously becoming a better person. Nice work!

TOUGH SHIFT turbulence is real. For every TOUGH SHIFT Event encountered, review and renew your answers to the

7 TOUGH SHIFT Questions. When your days are the darkest and most lonely, recognize the downward spiral and boldly begin your revitalization by acknowledging, "Oh, it's just a TOUGH SHIFT." 😉

TOUGH SHIFT Acknowledgments

Writing a book and creating related TOUGH SHIFT® programs and products is a group effort. Thanks to Tracey Jones and the Tremendous Leadership team for their partnership on producing and sharing this message. Amy Adams provided remarkable final copy edits and proofreading. Tim Schulte lent his expertise to the cover design. Two thumbs up to Anthony Raymond Michalski who graciously worked through the final production stages to get *TOUGH SHIFT* into to print.

Thanks to the team at On-Purpose Partners. Cheryl Anderson is our Integrator. Julie Holzmann excelled in her craft for the copy editing and proofreading of the original manuscript. Lori Moore joyfully keeps all online sites and carts working.

Thanks to Judith, my home team and bride since 1984. With her southern sensibilities, even she chuckled her support when I first told her all about "TOUGH SHIFT."

About Kevin W. McCarthy

Kevin is a lifelong student and practitioner of leadership principles and stewardship responsibilities, especially through the platform of business ownership. His first business, at age 9, was selling penny candy on the school bus. Since then, Kevin has continuously owned and operated businesses in commercial real estate, professional services, and publishing.

Kevin's experiences in business leadership and strategy produced On-Purpose®, an integrated approach to doing life and work well. His books *The On-Purpose Person: Making Your Life Make Sense* and *The On-Purpose Business Person: Doing More of What You Do Best More Profitably* are acclaimed, timeless best-selling modern parables. Because of his love of business, Kevin penned the iconoclastic book *Chief Leadership Officer: Increasing Wealth so Everyone Profits*.

Kevin serves as the Chief Leadership Officer and Founder of On-Purpose Partners—ONPURPOSE.*me*. He and Judith, his bride and Darden School classmate, have two adult children, Charles and Anne.